Manzovo

Place of the Elephants

Manzovo
Place of the Elephants

GARY ALBYN AND CRAIG BONE

For my children Adam and Paige
My greatest teachers

Gary Albyn
Johannesburg, South Africa
August 2008

My special thanks to Daniel 'Doc' Ellis, Anne-Marie Bone and Sean Bone
for their help with the illustrations

Craig Bone
Fort Myers, Fla, USA
August 2008

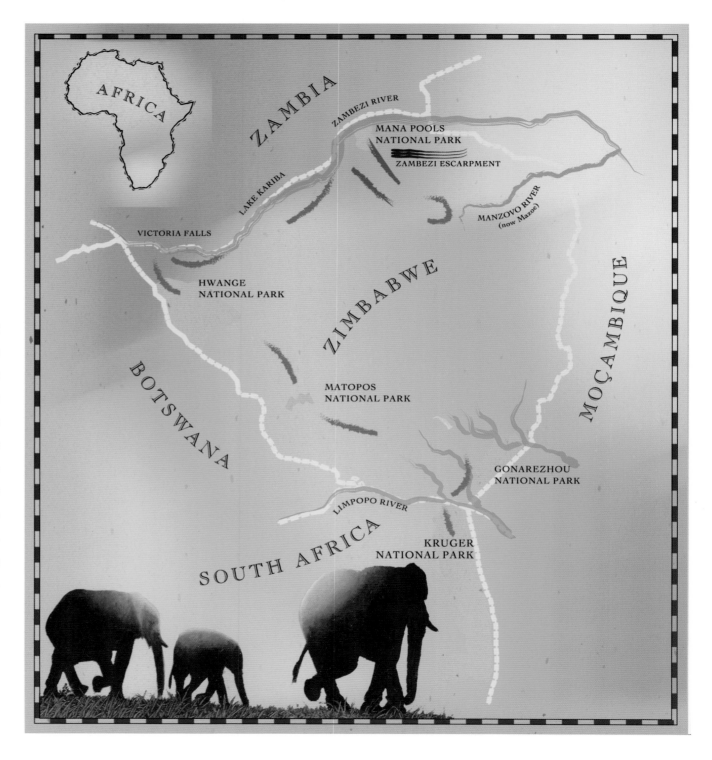

Note: Circa 1960, the time at which this story commences, the undertaking of such an odyssey would have been quite feasible for a herd of elephants. Fences encountered by transient herds would have provided little deterrence. Rural settlements, along with farmsteads, were thinly scattered at that time. Encroachments — usually opportunistic crop raids — would have been inflicted by nomadic herds.

After raising the Imperial flag at Fort Salisbury in 1890,
members of Cecil Rhodes' Pioneer Column wasted no time in relaying news
of the abundant riches and splendour of this 'new land' lying to the
north of the Limpopo. Along with their assortment of administrators
and assistants, this early regiment was soon followed by the more adventurous
prospectors, hunters and farmers. A cursory glance at the history of any
nascent colony will reveal the miraculous attraction such places hold for
pettifoggers, opportunists, mountebanks and the like. And so, amidst
this mélange, a hardy nation arose. For the next nine decades,
the country they helped forge was known as Rhodesia, before becoming
an independent Zimbabwe.

In the patriarchal style typical of the times, the colonial administrators
saw fit to anglicize many of those place names whose vernacular
pronunciations proved too taxing for their English tongues. Along with
many others, the name Manzovo was corrupted to the less spirantal version
Mazoe, by decree of the specially convened Geographical Names Committee.

Manzovo, deriving from one of the region's sub-dialects, translates to
'Place of the Elephants'.

FOREWORD

Gary Albyn's epic poem reached me at our Karkloof home on a brilliant sunny day. As I opened the envelope, a fish eagle called in the distance. Being my special bird, the synchronicity foretold of good omens. Our small farm lies at the foot of the great Karkloof forest which stretches from east to west for over thirty miles. As I began to read the poem, my imagination took flight.

When my ancestors – both Boer and British – arrived in Natal, the Karkloof forest and the wetlands of the valley saw the comings and goings of many hundreds of elephants. Today the wetlands have been drained but in the forest, young explorers often pick up remnants of tusks and teeth. There are stones too in the valley that have been rubbed smooth by generations of elephants. Gary Albyn's poem evokes a nostalgic and deep understanding of the plight of all wild animals in this great 'keep' we call the African wildlands. He does it through the metaphor of an elephant herd seeking a place

of refuge and one follows their journey wondering what tragedy is going to happen next.

I read on and was reminded of all the similarities that exist between Loxodonta africana and Homo sapiens. The poem instantly bonds us with this troubled band and verse by verse we follow their fortunes. There is something in the southern African soil that brings a moving lyrical quality to our writers of poetry and prose. Gary Albyn takes an honoured place in the list of our poets and writers. He writes from both the heart and the mind and it is obvious that he has watched many elephants in his time. No one who reads this epic poem can be unmoved about the plight of this 'Great Trek' of an elephant herd moving through the African landscape. It has become a too familiar story of what is happening to the wildlife of our continent, but it takes a poet of Albyn's stature to touch the deepest parts of your heart. I read the poem first silently and then out aloud, because when a poem is spoken there are nuances of emotion which cannot be experienced by silent reading. At the end of my second reading aloud I felt the tears beginning to brim and I knew that it is important for this poem to be read out aloud to attentive audiences.

I too have a great love of these wonderful animals, but I also have a deep respect and an equal amount of fear. Much of my life has been bound up with the rhinoceros and I recall many narrow escapes from charging black rhinos out on patrol, or on trail with my great friend and mentor, Magqubu Ntombela. He had a sixth sense and was able to anticipate what was likely to happen – a simple nod of his head indicated that you should immediately climb a tree! It is different with elephants; there is no point in climbing a tree because they can pluck you out like a ripe plum and kneel you to a pulp. I have observed the result of kneeling on a poor Amatonga man who tried to chase elephants away from his tiny patch of *m∂umbes* (tubers). It

was a ghastly sight, but it was also a reminder to treat this great animal with circumspection.

The sagacity of elephants is justifiably legendary and, in my own experience, I have seen acts of intelligence and courage that left me full of awe. In 1966, after taking a convoy of white rhinos from iMfolozi Game Reserve to Wankie (now Hwange) National Park, I accompanied some game rangers on an elephant capture. A young calf was darted but the mother refused to leave it. We fired shots over her head and into the ground near her, but she refused to move. Eventually a game ranger fired a Very pistol to drive her away. The flaming cartridge set the veld alight and to our amazement the mother stamped on the flames. Who can forget too the elephant breaking a branch and swiping hopelessly at a hovering helicopter carrying rangers who had just darted cows and calves in a small herd. The ability of elephants to communicate over long distances, at frequencies that we humans cannot hear, remains another mystery of this superb beast.

Gary Albyn writes about Kariba and mentions Fothergill. In 1961 I had the pleasure of meeting up with Rupert Fothergill on Lake Kariba when he was still rescuing animals from the small islands. I remember very clearly the way he spoke about elephants and how wonderful it was that they were more than capable of taking care of themselves and swimming long distances, helping each other. Gary Albyn has written a magnificent poem and it comes at a critical moment in the history of the country of his birth. Both elephants and human beings are undergoing the horrors of misguided politicians.

It is my fervent hope that the rulers of Zimbabwe will read this poem out aloud in the National Assembly, and in the schools, so that it will touch the hearts and the minds of people and bring about a transition of thought and deed and a realization that we are all children, mankind and animal, of the Great Continent of Africa.

Dr Ian Player, August 2008

While Dr Ian Player's myriad legacies are intricately woven into the fabric of South Africa's wildlife heritage, this bestselling author (of Zululand Wilderness, Shadow and Soul *and* The White Rhino Saga) *is an international colossus in the field of conservation. Ian Player was made a Knight in the Order of the Golden Ark by the late Prince Bernhard of The Netherlands and is the recipient of countless other honours, including the Gold Medal for Conservation from the San Diego Zoological Society.*

CONTENTS

Veiled through the mists of a new born day

A fiery disc in the east arising

Birds astir in the branches above

Greet the sun as it strikes the horizon

A river runs her ancient course

As Africa sheds its cape

The filtered rays dig through the gloom

Filmy outlines taking shape

20

It's a gruelling day for predator and prey

In this unfolding African drama

As the land awakens 'tween river and scarp

In the valley of Zambezi's Mana

Great Zambezi – serpent of jade

Flowing east through Mana Pools

Hollows swell when the river floods

Like quilts with embroidered jewels

Echoing faintly off distant cliffs

A fish eagle's cry is trilled

The morning rent by his strident call

Africa's essence distilled

The sight of a leopard's sinuous blur

Spreads gossip amongst resting vervets

She pays no heed to the chattering troop

Restoring calm amidst the nervous

Slowly stretching with feline grace

Eyes agleam like copper flowing

Lioness stands outside her den

Tawny cubs inside are growing

A curious face from its hole appears

Wary mongoose checks her surrounds

She'll venture forth if she thinks it's safe

Hungry prowlers are all around

A rippled wave begins to form

Down the length of a living fossil

A fearsome croc patrols the shore

For a sandbank he's sure to jostle!

Now lanced with shafts of dapple grey light

Outlines emerge from the murk

Imposing heads with enforcer's horn

Buffaloes prepare for work

New Arrival

Thandi stiffens as one more wave

Rises painfully deep within

Four births before – she knows the signs

A new life – ready to begin

She holds her bellow by force of will

Heaving hard as her muscles tighten

Drawing attention is ill advised

Alert scavenger's senses heightened

Hyena lurking with slavering grin

Prying menace around the fringes

His call unwelcome is met with a charge

From the mid-wife he darts and cringes

Exhausted now by her mammoth ordeal

Amniotic fluids start to surge

With slippery gush and unfolding sigh

Gossamer sac begins to emerge

Thandi brings her attention to bear

Relying on instincts primal

With tender coaxing and gentle nudge

She hails her latest arrival

The mid-wife attendant begins to scream

But a cry of pure benevolence

The herd awaits at the edge of the woods

Joyous news for anxious elephants

Encircling cows form a tight embrace

Expressing from temporal glands

The matriarch leads her small parade

Through glades and acacia stands

Like an empty vessel, Lesedi will learn

Naïve to her state of reliance

She'll mimic mother and minders alike

Emulating these peaceful giants

Fear

With a range as vast as Africa's plains

Thandi trusts her guiding instinct

Imprinted like road maps deep in her brain

Every feature quite distinct

But just like a river's ebb and flow

Thandi's herd observes a change

Each season they cross the endless plains

New outposts invade their range

Their urge to rove both far and wide

Is testing the farmers' patience

Crisp blond grass of the open plains

Replaced by juicy temptations

48

Scarecrows and fences have no effect

Harsh measures are then employed

Farmers resort to rifles and guns

Intruders, alas, destroyed

From south and east they test the wind

Man's caustic scent encroaches

But even in their haven wild

Their foremost fear is poachers

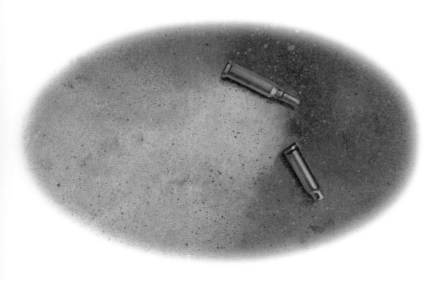

They've heard the crackle of distant guns

Rushing headlong t'other way

The decoy sprung by the poaching gang

In ambush the hunters lay

Pitching-on to the poachers' trap

Into volleys of lead and flame

Havoc and fear consumes the herd

A bloody killing field of shame

Four noble bulls now pay the price

Slain for a covetous fact

They twitch and heave in death's dark throes

As their tusks are crudely hacked

Searing their trunks with the stench of death

The foul scent on the wind is borne

Thandi must lead them away from here

This is no place to stop and mourn

For days she drives the elephants hard

Induced by anger and fear

The weak and weary are lagging back

Infants struggling in the rear

Their sanctuary lies beyond the scarp

Thandi drives the herd relentless

Confusion and loathing still cloud her brain

Images of slaughter senseless

Nyaminyami

Beyond the rise she will rest her herd

Recalling the river is near

Behold this sight – it's not quite right

What has happened to the cliffs so sheer?

Six seasons have passed since last she came

And she finds it difficult to fathom

The mighty river is boiling below

A massive wall now spans its chasm

Through the ages nomadic tribes

Were forced out by the tsetse fever

Livestock fell to the biting fly

Leaving pristine this place Kariba

From atop The Heights Thandi sees for miles

Reflections like shimmering jewels

Tentacles of water spread from the dam

Deep hollows become swollen pools

Trapped on islands by the rising tide

Little time for rescuers brave

Fothergill led the 'Noah Op'

Saving beasts from a watery grave

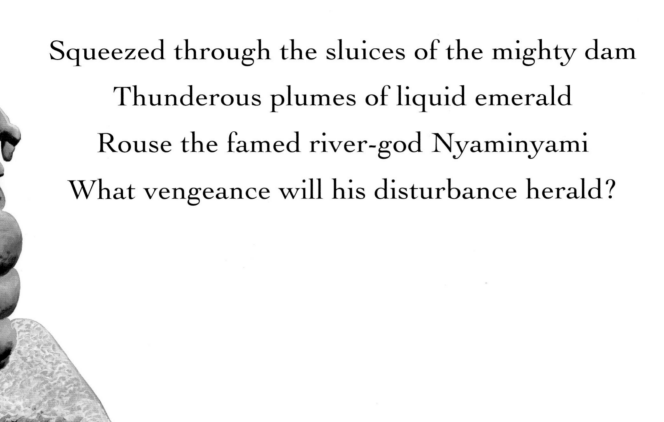

Squeezed through the sluices of the mighty dam

Thunderous plumes of liquid emerald

Rouse the famed river-god Nyaminyami

What vengeance will his disturbance herald?

Teenagers

Prospering now on the lake's southern shore

Two teens have completed their lessons

Soon they will join a bachelor herd

Moving on as they reach adolescence

Dawdling awkwardly beyond the herd

They tug aimlessly on a bush

Not quite sure of the world beyond

They await the predictable push

Out on the fringes they loiter unsure

Exiled by the rest of the herd

They struggle to sever the apron strings

Seeking attention quite absurd

Like hulking clowns at the river's edge

With inflated teenage swagger

Ends in a farce as the ledge subsides

Shame-faced by their clumsy stagger

They'll shadow the herd for a few more months

Needing time to build their bravado

Eager as they are to sever their ties

Still reluctant to go commando!

With a bachelor herd they'll soon unite

Carving paths through the open vistas

They'll range and trek over distances vast

Bolder than their mothers and sisters

Lesedi meanwhile has also matured

Nurturing her instincts maternal

Her role as nanny and minder alike

Fulfilling the process eternal

Odd Couples

The richness of life on Africa's plains

Like vaudeville is quite amusing

She watches absorbed as dramas unfold

Some relationships quite confusing

A honeyguide fussing has found a hive
In a stand of acacia trees
She pilots a badger right to the nest
He's immune to the African bees

But the badger breaks a cardinal rule

Leaving naught a drop of spoils

So the very next time she sings her tune

He's lured to the serpent's coils

Atop her nest at the water's edge

A plucky thick-knee guards her clutch

But a female croc with buried eggs

A neighbour – close enough to touch!

Each set-of-eggs would be a tasty treat

To a marauding river lizard

But alerting calls from the bird alarmed

Might just see the intruder scissored!

Mosi–oa–Tunya

Hugging the waters along the southern bank

The herd has been following the sun

Soon they're aware of an unusual sound

Like the vibrating skin of a drum

With sensitive ears they detect a sound

No human capable of hearing

A muted hum only they can perceive

On its source they now take a bearing

With trunks held aloft to sample the air

Each hoisted like a periscope

Curiously drawn to the constant roar

Bemused by the 'Thundering Smoke'

Soaring above on filigreed wings

Angels gaze at the 'Smoke and Thunder'

Circling over Victoria Falls

Also known as Mosi-oa-Tunya

The seething cauldron in the gorge below

Propels vapours high in the sky

As torrents of water come gushing down

Billowing mist banks formed on high

This constant deluge cascading down

Is a natural irrigation

Life abounds in the forest nearby

Like Eden in early creation

Thandi's alert to the presence of man

She watches in utter dismay

For along the village's narrow roads

Another herd gets right-of-way!

While she spies from afar – this smaller herd

Strolls nonchalantly down the street

Pedestrians scurry whilst drivers stop

Yet this herd need not be discreet

She ushers her herd along a path

Without fear nor sense of jeopardy

Soon they discover an object strange

It's Livingstone's famous effigy

Against the statue the elephants rub

The continent's daring visionary

Boldly outspoken of the trade in slaves

Africa's enduring missionary

Carnage

Leisurely browsing on succulent leaves

Their temperament quite relaxed

Tuned to the network of elephant sounds

A haven to the south attracts

Nature acts with balanced force

Where elephants generate growth

What may appear as wanton ruin

Is a pact that serves them both

A seed that travels right through their gut

Finds home in a fertile mound

Dung beetles busily roll their prize

Then bury them underground

But as their range is shrunk by man

In parks they find a sanctuary

If left unchecked with no controls

They lay bare the natural pantry

Despite its size, the Hwange Park

Can't hold this population

Those who study cause-and-effect

Believe in conservation

The scales tip as the growing herds

Destroy the vegetation

The roots no longer bind the soil

To sustain the population

Those who manage this delicate scheme

Must intervene to keep the balance

Controlling numbers by culling herds

A grisly task devoid of malice

An elephant's ears are extremely adept

So in the fiercest African heat

They effectively act as climate control

As they are waved to a rhythmic beat

They're also used for social gesture

As humans use body language

From jauntily cocked to folded flat

Signals joy right through to anguish

Working at frequencies below our own

Nuances only they detect

Elephants can both transmit and receive

Used to commune to great effect

With sensitive ears they clearly detect

Unmistakable mortal pangs

A distressing herd in a pincer move

Is surrounded by culling gangs

Swathed in fear the milling herd

Bellows in pure dismay

As rifles belch their gouts of flame

The cull gets underway

The clatter and boom of bullets fired

Mingles with the sounds of death

Soon the carcasses begin to pile

As the herd … loses … its … breath

A fetid taint on the wind aloft

As a bloodied veil is drawn

The sordid sounds have carried far

And the elephants begin to mourn

Amatoba

The herd is on the move again

They set a southerly bearing

Covering ground with rolling gait

The pace is cruel and wearying

Worn and weak from the brutal march

A refuge is soon revealed

'Tween serried domes of weathered rock

The elephants well concealed

This lonely place has a spectral feel

Enigmatic yet tranquil auras

Hear the wind and the echoing call …

Of the cries of ancient warriors

Zulu outcast, Mzilikazi king
A fearsome and imposing ruler
Presided over this mighty realm
Bequeathed to his son Lobengula

Under the regis of his battle shield

Dominion over all he led

Here in Matobo he settled his tribe

In Ndebele it means 'bald head'

Eerie, mysterious, secrets old
It trembles with arcane forces
Steeped with the blood of fallen men
Divined in the bones of sorcerers

Sighing on the breeze, fallen warriors chant

Ghostly echoes from history's pages

Murmurs from beyond to the mystic conveyed

Deciphering the wisdom of ages

For a lack of water the herd moves on

Thandi leaves this place so sacred

Without a mud bath to cover their hides

Their skin feels exposed and naked

An African Storm

A natural urge is pulling them south

And the herd obeys instinctive

They soon reach Sabi and Gonarezhou

Cliffs of Chilojo distinctive

The dry Limpopo's thirsty sands

Swallow each torpid puddle

Converging spoor around the pools

Show where the wretched huddle

The terrain is arid all is parched

The weaker ones ready to die

When Nature's dowsers come ambling by

Opening wells when all is dry

The elephants scan horizons far

For a hint of woolly cumulus

Behold this sight – an African storm

Tempestuous forces furious

The bush is brittle and the rains are late

A looming storm-front full of promise

Roiling warriors throw spears of light

From soaring anvils black and ominous

The air is tight with electric charge

Then split by a luminous bolt

Bloated raindrops start a Morse attack

Chased by an acoustic assault

The raging river now bursts its banks

As the sodden seek out a refuge

Carcasses churn in the swollen flood

Swept away in the tumbling deluge

150

Dormant codes locked deep in their cells

React to the recent showers

Sap diffused through osmotic force

Nourishes the buds and flowers

The animals thrive and drop their calves

Making good in times of plenty

Drought is common on Africa's plains

And the pools could soon be empty

Hercules vs Antaeus

What primal force now pulls them south

Across Limpopo's channels?

The Kruger Park holds great allure

This place of birds and mammals

Ancient baobabs claw at the sky

Their branches like broken fingers

Yield their bounty to man and beast

Such that life around them hinges

God told hyena to plant the first tree

It wasn't a difficult chore

But instead it was planted upside-down

According to legend and lore!

Lesedi's matured and seeks a mate

Shameless suitors gather her scent

Eager to sate a primal urge

They send signals of lustful intent

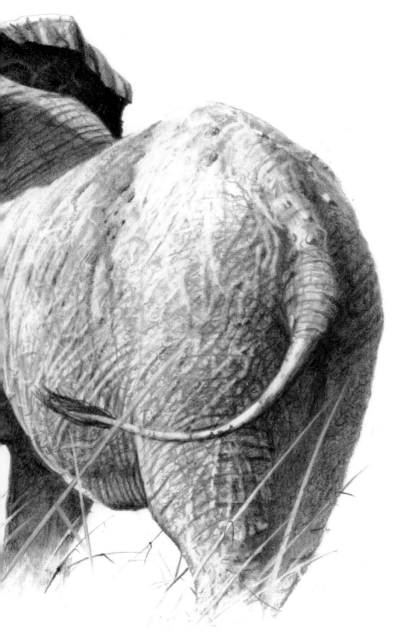

Two of the bulls are now in musth
Each of them grand and colossal
Their hormones rage and juices flow
Like titans begin to jostle

With thunderous force two bulls collide

Hercules versus Antaeus

They rage and wrestle but neither gives

Amidst fury, noise and chaos

Angled beams of broken light

Explode through clouds of dust

Glimpses brief of warring beast

The sound of clashing tusk

A vicious thrum vibrates the air

The drama builds supreme

Quivering trees let loose their leaves

The fighters charge and scream

Ivories rattle like flashing swords

As they wrangle, parry and slash

A frenzied mass of sinew and bone

As the duelling elephants clash

One soon weakens and yields an inch

The other presses the attack

Whips his trunk with a mighty sweep …

The vanquished finally steps back

Darwin's assertion is true no doubt

With the fittest, females breed

Progeny receive the best of genes

The victor's dominant seed

The Legacy

Lesedi is ready to drop her calf

The foetus now stretches her womb

An elephant carries the longest term

That's twenty-two phases of moon

She presents her calf to the waiting herd

Always a joyous occasion

But as one life starts … another must end

Nature's eternal equation

Thandi has lost her battle with age

Lesedi must now take the lead

The matriarch's teeth are worn and flat

She can no longer browse and feed

So it is that an epoch ends

A legacy etched on the plains

But Thandi's wisdom will endure

Long after her mortal remains

What lasting legacy will we bestow?

Little, considering our history

Generations hence, appalled by our greed

Will quail at our confounding mystery

184

Our fragile blue island is withering away

We are rolling the dice on our chances

For each living system we greedily destroy

We collectively lose vital answers

The Earth apparatus is choking to death

But our indifference has no ending

Each generation owes a debt in advance

To the future our youth should be spending

We ascribe to ourselves, the lofty task

We're our planet's supposed attendants

So long as we allow the ceaseless rape …

Are we indeed the species ascendant?

ACKNOWLEDGEMENTS

As with any collaborative project, none of this would have been possible without the unstinting advice, encouragement and assistance of many people. I offer my sincere thanks for their invaluable contributions, in whatever form they may have taken. It is possible that I might have missed some names and I can only hope they will forgive the oversight.

Craig Bone is an extraordinarily talented artist with a hard-earned reputation. My imaginary musings, a full two years prior to making contact and securing his commitment, visualized him as the book's eventual illustrator. To paraphrase Benjamin Zander, never doubt the Art of Possibility.

Agonizing over whether a book gets printed or not is the domain of the publisher. My eternal thanks go to Chris and Kerrin at 30° South Publishers for not only sharing my dream, but liberating hidden potentials within *Manzovo*.

Alan MacIsaac, wordsmith and mentor, has been dispensing his avuncular advice for decades. Scornful of mediocrity, his influence has been immeasurable.

With his trademark tenacity and indefatigable zeal, Dr Ian Player's legacies reverberate throughout the conservation community. It is a true privilege having him write the foreword.

Like the principal 'character' in *Manzovo*, Lisette is not dissimilar to Thandi – a true matriarch in every respect. Never short of love, advice and encouragement, she is a tireless virago. Along with Ian and especially Greg, they have taught me much about elephants and the need to preserve our heritage.

My gratitude goes to John and Tebogo, both skilled professionals, for breathing life into the recording of *Manzovo*. Hugely experienced in the arcane craft of design and layout, Marlene waved her magic wand over the book.

I reserve special thanks for my trusted friends Ian, Phil and Gail, James and Grayboy, and of course numerous others – too many to mention – for their encouragement throughout the project.

To my parents, wife and children, upon whose abundant love, support – and oftentimes tolerance of my mystifying adventures – I can always depend! You remain the bedrock in my life.

Gary Albyn
Johannesburg, South Africa
August 2008
www.manzovo.co.za

Published in 2008 by Southbound
An imprint of 30° South Publishers (Pty) Ltd.
28, Ninth Street, Newlands, 2092
Johannesburg, South Africa
www.30degreessouth.co.za
info@30degreessouth.co.za

Design and origination by Marlene Willoughby-Smith
Map by Marlene Willoughby-Smith
Audio CD produced by Southbound

Printed and bound by Pinetown Printers, Durban

ISBN 9781920143220